Three World Religions

Contents

There are many religions in the world.
They teach people how to live.

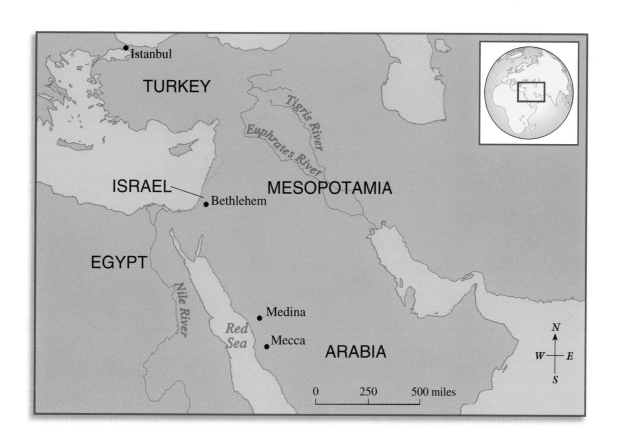

Today this part of the world is called the Middle East.
Three world religions started here.

The Torah is written in Hebrew.
It is kept in a special place in Jewish houses
of worship.

Jewish houses of worship are called temples
or synagogues.
This synagogue is in Jerusalem.

The Bible says that long ago, Jews were slaves in Egypt.
They had to build cities for the pharaohs.

One pharaoh ordered that all Jewish baby
boys should be drowned in the Nile River.
The mother of Moses wanted to save him.

The Bible says that one day Moses heard God speak from a burning bush.
God's voice told him to free the Jewish slaves.

The pharaoh would not free the Jewish slaves.
God punished the pharaoh and his country.

The Bible says that the Red Sea parted so
that the Jews could escape.
The pharaoh's army could not follow them.

Jews celebrate Hanukkah by lighting candles. The candles are a symbol of a miracle that happened long ago.

There are many Christians around the world.
They go to many different churches.

Christians believe in Jesus Christ. The story of Jesus is told in the New Testament of the Bible.

Christians believe that Jesus died and rose again. The cross and the lily are symbols of the Christian religion.

Christmas is a happy holiday.
It celebrates the birth of Jesus.

The Bible says that three kings came to Bethlehem.
They brought presents to the baby Jesus.

People gathered around Jesus when he talked about the laws of God.
He told them about the Golden Rule.

This famous painting is called the Last Supper.
It shows Jesus with his disciples.

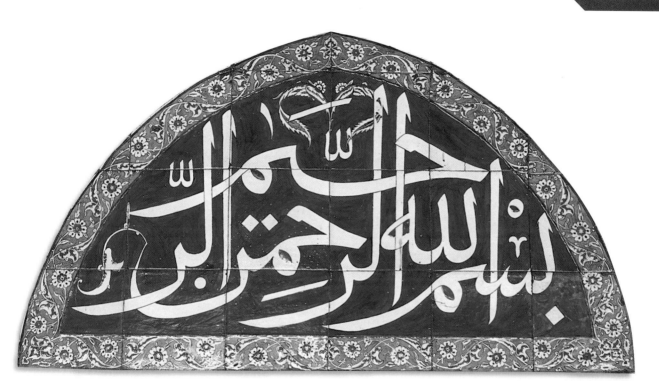

Allah means God in the Arabic language.
These sacred words say that God is merciful.

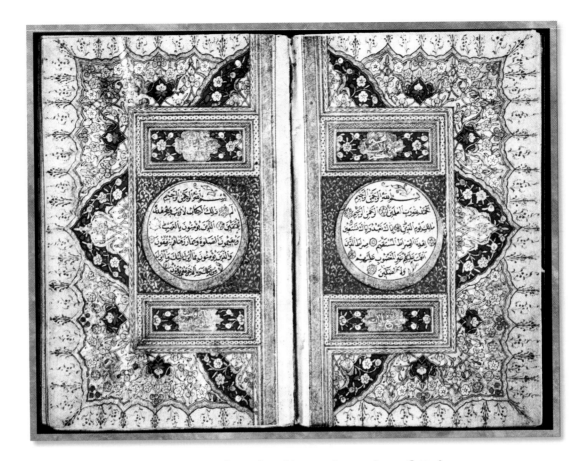

The Koran is the holiest book of Islam. Muslims believe that the Koran is the word of Allah.

Muslims live all over the world.
Some Muslims live in the United States.
These Muslim girls live in a country in Asia.

Muslims must pray five times a day.
On Fridays, they go to a mosque to pray.

Mecca is the holiest city of Islam.
All Muslims try to go there at least once.
This picture shows the Kaaba.

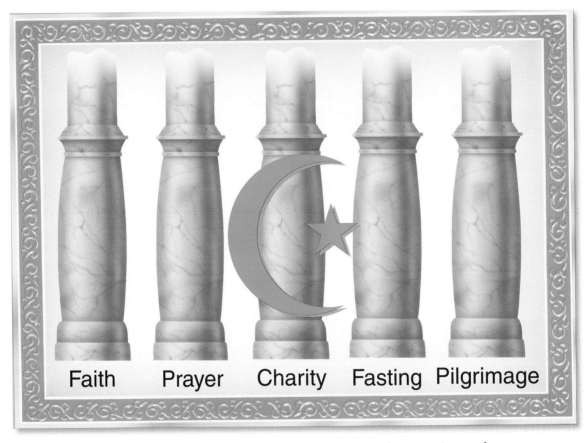

Faith　Prayer　Charity　Fasting　Pilgrimage

There are five very important laws in Islam.
Every Muslim must follow these laws.
They are called the Five Pillars.